WHEN THE WORLD BEGAN

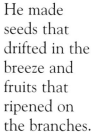

In the beginning it was very, very dark. There was no light at all.

Then God said, "Let there be light!" and suddenly there was light. God divided the light from the darkness and made day and night. Then he divided the sky above from the earth below, and he was pleased with what he'd done.

On the earth there were swirling waters and crashing waves, huge seas and mighty rivers. God sorted out the water from the land, and the hills from the valleys.

The world began to take shape.

Then God began to make the flowers and trees, and everything that grows. He made giant trees with green leaves, and tiny flowers with blue petals.

He made seeds that drifted in the breeze and fruits that ripened on the branches.

God made millions and millions of stars and planets, comets and asteroids. Some stars were huge, others were tiny. But each one had a special place in space.

Then he made the sun to shine in the day, and the moon for the dark night sky.

God also made all sorts of creatures. Duck and deer, ants and elephants – they really did look beautiful. He made the crocodile and the hippo, the baboon and the bushbaby. He made the python and the porcupine, the flying fish and the croaking frog.

He made animals with hooves and animals with humps. Some had long tails, others had short ones. Many had no tails at all.

One or two had really fantastic tails. They were the show-offs!

When God had finished with all the animals he made two very special people.

God made a man called Adam and a woman called Eve.

Adam and Eve thought the world was beautiful.

There was nothing to beat it!

ADAM AND EVE

In the beginning, when the world was new, God made a beautiful garden for the people he had made. It was full of wonderful trees and plants and amazing animals, bright butterflies and fabulous fishes.

Adam and Eve were very happy. They talked with God every day. They were his special friends.

"Eat anything you like," said God, "except from that tree, the tree of the knowledge of Good and Evil."

But lurking in the garden was God's enemy, the serpent. He whispered to Eve, "God didn't really mean it. If you eat that fruit, you will be clever... as clever as God!"

The moment Eve ate it, she knew she had disobeyed God. She gave some to Adam. He took a bite, then he said, "I don't think we should have done this."

All of a sudden Adam and Eve began to feel guilty and ashamed.

They ran to the bushes and tried to hide. They were worried that God might see them and know they had eaten the fruit. Adam and Eve were scared.

When God came to the garden at the end of the day he looked for his two special friends.

"Where are you?" he asked. God already knew that both Adam and Eve had disobeyed him by eating the fruit from the special tree.

Adam spoke from behind a bush. "We were hiding from you," he stammered. "We were ashamed because we had no clothes on."

"Who told you about needing clothes?" said God. "Have you eaten the fruit I told you not to eat?"

Eve spoke in a trembling voice. "The serpent made me do it," she said.

God turned to the serpent. "From this moment you will be hated by everyone, and you will have to crawl on the ground," he said.

God was sad. Adam and Eve had spoiled his garden and he would have to send them away. From now on their life would be difficult. God made clothes for them, and they left the garden. An angel guarded the gate.

But God already had a plan for making things right again. He would help all people to find their way back to him – as long as they wanted to.

It would take a long time... but God is very patient.

GOD'S PROMISE TO ABRAHAM

Before long, Abraham had things to worry about. There was not enough to eat in the new land, which was called Canaan, and everybody was hungry. So they trekked into Egypt, where there was plenty of corn. Abraham and Lot bought all the food they needed, but it didn't feel like home.

They left Egypt and travelled back to Canaan, and started to explore the land.

When Abraham was seventy-five years old, he started out on a long, long journey. He left his home, and set off for a new land, led by God. He went because God told him to, and Abraham trusted God.

Abraham took with him Sarah, his wife, and his nephew Lot. He also took all his possessions, his sheep and goats and cattle, and all his servants. God promised Abraham that his family would become a great nation in the new land, even though at the time Abraham didn't have any children.

As they stood on a high hill overlooking the country God had given him, Abraham realised that he and Lot now had so many sheep and cattle that there would not be enough land for them all to graze upon.

"We'd better split up," Abraham said to Lot. "You choose one way, and I'll go the other." Lot chose the land which was all green and grassy, the best land on the plains. Abraham went into the rocky hills of Canaan.

Abraham and Sarah were sad because they had no children, but one night God told Abraham that he would have lots of descendants. God told Abraham to look up into the night sky and count the stars. One day, he said, it would be just as hard to count all the people in Abraham's family!

Abraham was God's friend, and he often heard God speaking to him. The years passed, and Abraham and Sarah still had no children. But God reminded him, "Your name is Abraham, which means 'father of many'."

One hot day, when Abraham was sitting in the doorway of his tent, he was visited by three mysterious strangers. As was the custom, Abraham gave them something to eat and drink and waited to hear the reason for their visit. They told Abraham that in a year's time, he would have a child of his own.

Sarah burst out laughing. She just could not believe she would be a mother now! But Abraham had waited for this moment, and God amazed them both. A year later, Sarah had a baby. They called him Isaac, which meant laughter!

Abraham couldn't think how God's promise could come true. After all, he and Sarah were very old. But Abraham trusted God. And he waited.

Abraham and Sarah had seen a lot of sad things in their lives. They had even seen whole cities destroyed because of the cruel things people had been doing to one other. But nothing could shake Abraham's faith that God would keep his promise and give him a child.

Abraham was thrilled. So was Sarah. God had kept his promise. Even though he was old, Abraham could see that through Isaac, and Isaac's children, and his children's children, he was going to be the father of many people.

ESAU AND JACOB

Esau and Jacob were twins, but they were not at all alike. Esau, the elder son, was an outdoor man, a hairy hunter. Jacob, the younger, liked to stay at home, and he had smooth skin. It was easy to tell them apart.

Their father, Isaac, was an old man. He knew that God had great plans for both his sons, but he loved Esau best. Their mother, Rebecca, also had a favourite son. She loved Jacob best.

Jacob saw how much his father loved Esau.

One day, while Esau was out hunting, Jacob made a delicious stew.

Esau came home exhausted and hungry. "Give me some stew," he begged. "I'd give anything for a mouthful!"

"Anything?" asked Jacob. "Even your inheritance when our father dies?"

"Yes! Yes!" agreed Esau.

"OK then!" grinned Jacob. The deed was done.

14

Rebecca had heard the boys talking and smiled to herself. Now her favourite son would gain everything when his father died.

Eventually Isaac became frail and blind, and he thought he would die soon. He called Esau to his side and asked him to go hunting so that he could have a final meal. He promised he would give his blessing to Esau before he died.

The old man loved to eat the wild game caught by his son. So Esau took his bow and arrow and went out to hunt as his father had asked.

He was cunning and patient, a clever hunter.

Their mother Rebecca had overheard Isaac's request. Now Jacob could take his chance! She tied goat-skins to Jacob's arms and neck so that he would feel like Esau.

Then she gave Jacob a pot of delicious food and sent him in to see Isaac. She knew that, now the old man was blind, he could not see which of his sons was in his tent.

Esau knelt down by Isaac's side. He wept and pleaded with his father for a blessing of his own.

The old man was heartbroken but there was nothing he could do to change things. Once a blessing had been given, it could not be taken away.

Esau was so angry he promised to kill Jacob. But Jacob ran away from home. He stayed with his uncle and worked for him for many years.

Both Jacob and Esau had done things that were wrong, but later Jacob asked God to help him change his ways and learn to do the things that pleased God. Over the years God changed Jacob.

Isaac was surprised Esau had returned from hunting so quickly. He began to wonder whether it was Jacob who had come in to see him. But he stretched out his hand and felt the hairy skin.

"Are you really Esau?" he asked.

"I am!" lied Jacob.

Still unsure, Isaac asked for some food. Then the father laid his hand on Jacob's head and gave him his blessing. This meant Jacob – not Esau – would be the head of the family after his father's death. When Esau returned he discovered that he had been cheated out of his father's final blessing. He was furious!

When Jacob and Esau met again many years later, they were both older and wiser, and God helped them to be friends once more.

17

JOSEPH THE FAVOURITE

Jacob gave Joseph a special coat. None of his other sons had such a beautiful coat, and when the brothers saw it, they were jealous.

Joseph used to tell tales about his brothers. He told his father when they did not look after the sheep carefully enough. Joseph's brothers did not like him very much!

Jacob was an old man, and a very happy man. He had had four wives, and he had twelve fine sons.

Joseph and his younger brother, Benjamin, were the sons of Rachel, the wife Jacob loved best of all. He loved all his sons dearly, but Joseph was his favourite.

It didn't help when he told his brothers about his dreams. In the first dream Joseph imagined his brothers like sheaves of corn, all bowing down in front of him.

In the second dream Joseph saw the sun, the moon and eleven stars, all bowing down to him. "We're not going to bow down to you," his brothers said angrily.

One day,
the older brothers
took their sheep and goats to graze a long way off. Their father sent Joseph to see if they were all right. When the brothers saw Joseph in the distance, they said, "Here comes the dreamer!"

Suddenly, they were all furious.
"Who does he think he is?" they mutte
One of them said, "Let's kill him and t
him in a pit."
"Yes," said another, "let's say a wild an
has killed him!"

Then, to try to cover things up, they dipped Joseph's coat in goat's blood, and took it back to Jacob their father.
When they showed him the coat, he cried.
"He must have been killed by a wild animal," sobbed Jacob, heartbroken. His favourite son was dead.

But when Reuben, the eldest brother, heard their plans, he said, "Throw him in the pit by all means, but do not kill him!"

He planned to go back later to rescue Joseph. Then he went off to look after the sheep.

Some of the brothers stripped off Joseph's special coat and threw him into a big hole in the ground. He couldn't climb out. Then they saw some traders passing by on their way to Egypt, and the brothers decided they would sell Joseph as a slave.

Far away in Egypt, God looked after Joseph. He soon got a job as a slave for a man called Potiphar, the captain of the king's guard.

It wasn't much fun being a slave in a strange land instead of a rich man's son, but Joseph worked hard, and his master treated him well.

Soon Potiphar knew he could trust Joseph completely and so he put him in charge of everything.

But one day, someone told lies about Joseph, and before long… But that's another story!

21

JOSEPH THE PRISONER

Joseph was in a fix. He was a long way from his home and family. He was in prison for something he hadn't done. And although he knew that God was looking after him, he had no idea how he was going to get out.

Joseph was an Israelite, one of God's people, and he had worked as a slave for an important Egyptian called Potiphar. But, because someone had told lies about Joseph, he had been sent to prison.

Before long Joseph proved himself so trustworthy that the prison guard allowed him to look after the other prisoners. They all knew Joseph as their friend.

Joseph knew that God was with him, even in prison.

One day Joseph met two special prisoners: Pharaoh's butler and Pharaoh's baker. They had both upset Pharaoh and now they were paying the price. They had both had vivid dreams, and asked Joseph the meaning of them.

"Only God can give a person understanding of dreams," said Joseph. "Tell them to me."

"I dreamed," said the butler, "of a grapevine with three branches. I squeezed the grapes into Pharaoh's cup and gave it to him to drink. What does it mean?"

Joseph smiled. "Good news," he said. "In three days' time you'll have your old job back, serving wine to Pharaoh!"

The butler was as pleased as could be. He was impressed with Joseph.

"When you return to Pharaoh, could you please tell him about me?" asked Joseph. "I'm in prison but I've done nothing wrong."

"Certainly!" said the butler, humming to himself.

Then the baker asked Joseph to explain his dream.

"I was carrying three baskets on my head, with special cakes for Pharaoh in the top one. But on my way to him, some birds came and gobbled them up!" he said. "Will I be free in three days, too?"

Joseph looked very serious, sighed deeply, and said, "I am very sorry. The three baskets do mean three days, but at the end of three days you will be executed – and there is nothing I can do to prevent it."

Sadly for the baker, Joseph's words came true.

The butler was released. He returned to his old job and soon he forgot all about prison. He also forgot all about Joseph... until one day, two years later, Pharaoh had some dreams.

"I am told that God helps you explain dreams," said Pharaoh.

Joseph looked Pharaoh in the eye. "God says there will be seven good harvests, and then seven years of famine," he answered.

Pharaoh was staggered as Joseph continued, "Find someone who can organise your grain stores, and make sure the food is shared out fairly."

He called for all his wise men and magicians, and began to tell them what he had dreamed. "Can anyone tell me what it means?" pleaded Pharaoh. And he told them his dreams.

"There were seven fat cows by a river, and seven thin cows came and swallowed them up! Then I saw seven fat ears of corn, eaten up by seven thin ears of corn!" said Pharaoh.

Suddenly the butler thought of Joseph – still in prison. "Send for him!" ordered Pharaoh. So Joseph was washed and scrubbed and given new clothes and taken to meet Pharaoh.

Almost immediately, Pharaoh replied, "As God has shown my dream to you so clearly, you are the man for the job! Here's a ring as a sign of my authority. I'm putting you in charge!"

Before long Joseph was looking after all of Egypt. He served Pharaoh faithfully and well, but he never forgot he was an Israelite, one of God's people.

And, some time later, Joseph's prayers were answered. His father Jacob, and all of his brothers, came to live in Egypt, and they were reunited. The past was forgiven.

THE BABY IN THE BASKET

Many years after the death of Joseph, the Israelites were still living in Egypt. It was not their home and sometimes they wondered if they would ever go back to the land which God had given them. Pharaoh, the king of Egypt, treated the Israelites as slaves, and they worked all day long under the hot sun.

But Pharaoh was worried. Each year more and more Israelite babies were born. One day there might be so many Israelites that they would overrun his land. So he ordered his people to throw any newborn Israelite baby boys into the River Nile.

The Israelites were terrified. They did all they could to protect their children. One mother hid her baby son for three months, then she made a waterproof basket, just big enough to hide him in, and placed the little child in the basket by the reeds at the side of the river.

The baby's sister, Miriam, hid on the river bank and bravely watched the precious basket. She knew that if anyone caught her or

found the baby, she would be in deep trouble.

The princess said that as soon as the baby was old enough, she would adopt him, and take him to live with her at the palace. And so Moses, as he was called, went to live with the princess and was brought up by her.

Although he was brought up in an Egyptian palace, Moses never forgot he was an Israelite. He did not know that God had a plan to use him to lead his people out of Egypt, into the Promised Land.

Later the princess of Egypt and her friends were walking by the river, preparing to take a bath. Miriam watched as the princess spied the mysterious basket. Moments later the princess was cuddling the child. "It's a little Israelite baby!" she said.

Then Miriam did something very brave. She came out of her hiding place and said, "Would you like someone to help you look after that baby?"

The princess was delighted, so Miriam went to fetch her mother, and soon the little baby was being nursed by his real mother. The princess had no idea that this was the baby's mother and offered to pay her to look after the child.

27

Although Moses was brought up by an Egyptian princess, he never forgot that he had been born an Israelite. God's people, the Israelites, were slaves in Egypt. They were badly treated. But Moses knew that God had a special plan for his people.

When Moses grew up he left Egypt and settled in the land of Midian where he became a shepherd.

One day, on Mount Sinai, he saw a bush that seemed to be on fire. He moved nearer to look more closely, and saw that although the bush was burning, the fire was not destroying it.

Then Moses heard his name being called. He trembled. He knew it was the voice of God.

God said, "Moses, don't come any closer. Take off your sandals. You are standing on holy ground!"

God told Moses that it was time for the Israelite people to be freed from their slavery. And Moses was the man who would lead them.

Moses was terrified. "What shall I say if anyone asks me about this?" he trembled.

"Just say that I AM has sent you!" said God.

Moses didn't think he could do what God asked, but God promised to help him and told Moses to take his brother Aaron with him.

Moses returned to Egypt. There he saw how badly the Israelites were treated by the Egyptian slave-drivers. They were whipped and beaten, and they could not free themselves from slavery.

Moses and Aaron went to the palace, and said, "Let God's people go back to their own country, otherwise terrible things will happen in Egypt."

"I will not let them go," said Pharaoh.

Next came swarms of locusts which ate everything. Then darkness came for three whole days.

Still Pharaoh refused to let the Israelites go, so God told Moses his final plan. The Israelites must mark their doorposts with blood from a lamb, and they would be safe from harm. The Angel of Death would pass over their houses.

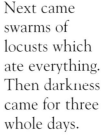

"If you don't let the people go," said Moses, "more terrible things will happen."

There were plagues of frogs, hordes of gnats, swarms of flies. Animals started to die, the people came out in terrible boils, and there was a violent hailstorm which destroyed most of the trees and all of the crops.

And so it was that all the rivers turned to blood. Many of the fish died. The smell was terrible! But Pharaoh still would not let the Israelites go.

But, despite all this, Pharaoh would not let them go.

"You're asking for trouble!" said Moses.

That night, the eldest child and animal of every Egyptian family died. This was too much for Pharaoh. Finally, he gave in.

"Go!" he wailed to Moses and Aaron. "And take your people with you."

The Israelites were free at last. They collected together their belongings and left Egypt with Moses as their leader.

Then they began their long journey to the land God had promised them.

ESCAPE FROM EGYPT

The Israelites were trapped! Fear rippled through the camp. Ahead were the waters of the Red Sea; behind them, the Egyptian chariots. Had God rescued them from slavery in Egypt, only to let them die?

Moses did not panic. He listened to God. As he stretched out his hand, a strong wind blew – and a dry pathway appeared. The Israelites crossed over safely to the other side.

As the waters returned, the Egyptians, with their army of chariots, were drowned. The Israelites were free! No longer slaves in Egypt, they were on th way to the Promised Land.

Moses and his brother Aaron thanked God. Their sister Miriam and the other women sang and danced.

When the Israelites came to Mount Sinai, God spoke to Moses. "Tell the people: if you obey me, I promise that you will be my special people. I will give you laws so that you can worship me." And God gave them the Ten Commandments.

Everybody stood back from the mountain in awe as a thick cloud came down. Thunder rumbled, lightning flashed, the ground shook. And Moses climbed the mountain to meet God.

After a time, the people got tired of waiting. They went to Aaron, saying, "Let's make a god we can worship down here."

They took off their gold jewellery to make a calf, like one of the Egyptian gods. They thanked it for bringing them out of Egypt. Then they had a party.

But before long, the singing and dancing turned to grumbling. "We wish we had died in Egypt," the people said. "We will starve to death in this desert."

Then God promised: "I will make bread rain down from heaven." And each night, manna fell from the sky like frost, and each morning the Israelites gathered enough food for one day.

Sometimes it was hard to find water. The Israelites went to Moses and grumbled. "Give us water," they said, "or we'll kill you."

Moses asked God, "What shall I do?"

"Take your stick and hit the rock," said God. So Moses did as God told him, and fresh water streamed out.

God sent Moses down the mountain. Moses was furious when he remembered God's first law: "I am the Lord your God. You shall not have any other gods but me."

Then Moses was sad. "O God, forgive them!" he pleaded. And he destroyed the golden calf.

Some of the Israelites still wanted to be God's special people. And they were sorry.

At last the day came when the Israelites could see Canaan, the Promised Land. Moses sent twelve men to spy out the land. When they reported back, Joshua and Caleb were excited. "It's a land of plenty," they said.

But the other ten spies said, "There are giants living there; the cities have huge walls. We'd never be able to beat them."

Because his people would not trust God, the Israelites had to wander through the desert for the next forty years, instead of going into the Promised Land.

From the top of Mount Nebo, Moses saw the Promised Land once before he died. Joshua was the new leader of God's people.

THE PROMISED LAND

The fortress-city of Jericho towered above the plain. Its walls were high, its gates were strong, its army was ready, but its inhabitants were terrified – of the Israelites.

The River Jordan was in flood, the waters whirling and surging as they tumbled downstream. But God's people did exactly what Joshua told them, so that at last, all the people crossed over the Jordan into the land that God had promised them.

When the king of Jericho heard there were spies in the city, he sent soldiers to catch them. But a woman called Rahab hid the men under a pile of flax on the roof of her house in the city walls.

"Everyone knows that your God can do miracles," said Rahab. "Remember me and my family when you capture Jericho."

Then Rahab helped the men escape by a rope let down from her window.

Joshua waited for his spies to return, and then he told the people, "God will do amazing things tomorrow."

On the other side of the River Jordan, Joshua and the Israelites were ready for action.

Joshua heard God's voice, "Don't be afraid, because I am with you." First, Joshua sent two of his men to Jericho. "Spy out the land," he said, "and find out as much as you can."

Jericho lay ahead, its gates firmly shut. But God had a plan. It did not involve huge armies or battering rams; it depended on the Israelites obeying his instructions.

"First, march round the walls once a day for seven days." So the Israelites did what they were told.

God spoke to Joshua again.

"On the seventh day, march round the city seven times – and when the priests blow their trumpets, all of you must shout."

And when the Israelites shouted on that seventh day, the walls of Jericho fell down! Only Rahab and her family were saved.

From that day, God was with the Israelites as they took control of Canaan, city by city.

The twelve tribes of Israel settled in the land God had promised them. And God was their king.

One night, God spoke to Samuel. At first he thought it was Eli calling him, but Eli knew who it was.

"Listen carefully," said Eli. And so Samuel learned to listen to God.

Before he was born, Samuel's mother knew that God had chosen him to do special work for him.

As a young boy, Samuel lived at the temple in Shiloh, taught by Eli the old priest.

By the time Samuel was grown up, the people of Israel had forgotten God's laws and had started to worship other gods.

Their enemies, the Philistines, kept beating them in battle, and then they stole the special box containing God's laws.

SAMUEL LISTENS TO GOD

When Samuel prayed for the people, they were sorry. "We will serve God," they said, "and we will listen to him."

Then everything went wrong for the Philistines. Terrified, they put the special box on an ox-cart and sent it back – with no driver! After that, there was peace.

When Samuel was an old man, the people asked for a king.

"God is your king," said Samuel, but the people would not listen. So God told Samuel to anoint Saul – a young man, handsome and tall – as king over Israel.

At first, all went well. Samuel gave King Saul advice and the king obeyed God. But soon Saul decided he did not need Samuel's advice or God's help – and after a while Samuel warned Saul that God would choose another king.

And so Samuel went to Bethlehem and secretly anointed David, a shepherd boy, to be Israel's next king.

Samuel prayed that David would obey God and lead his people to worship him always.

When Samuel died, all God's people were sad, including Saul. The next time Saul needed Samuel's advice, Samuel wasn't there to help him.

37

DAVID AND GOLIATH

David was puzzled. "Why are you so scared of a man like that who doesn't even believe in God?" he asked.

"What do you know about battles?" replied one of David's brothers angrily.

But David could not understand why all the Israelites were so afraid. After all, God was on their side.

David the shepherd boy had walked many miles to the camp where the Israelite army was preparing for battle with the Philistines. David's brothers were soldiers, and their father had sent David with food for them. He wanted to know how they were, and he hoped David would return with some good news.

But when David arrived, it was bad news. The Israelite soldiers were terrified of the Philistine champion. David hurried to find his brothers.

"What's going on?" he asked.

They explained that everyone was terrified by the Philistine giant, Goliath. He was nearly nine feet tall, wore massive armour and carried a huge sword. Every day he came out to jeer at the Israelite army, and no one was brave enough, or strong enough, to fight him.

Soon everyone heard about the boy who was not afraid of Goliath, and before long David was standing before King Saul.

"I'll fight Goliath," said David boldly. "I've fought off lions and bears with my catapult while looking after my sheep. God has always kept me safe before. He will help me now."

King Saul was amazed at David's courage. He decided to let him fight Goliath, and he offered him his finest armour and sharpest sword.

David strapped on the armour and lifted the sword. But it was all too heavy and awkward for him. He took it off again.

"These are what I need," said David, holding five smooth stones and his catapult. Then he went to meet Goliath.

Goliath laughed. "Do you think I'm a dog, scaring me away with sticks and stones?" he said. Everyone watching was terrified... except David.

"You may have weapons," David shouted, "but I've got the living God on my side."

Carefully, David hurled a stone at the giant. It struck Goliath on the forehead, and he crashed to the ground, dead.

A great cheer went up from the Israelites, while the Philistines turned and ran. David had defeated a mighty army. But David knew that he had not beaten Goliath. God himself had done it.

DAVID THE KING

After King Saul was killed in battle, David became king. Years before, when he was a boy, the prophet Samuel had anointed him. And now David wanted to be a good and fair ruler of God's people. He prayed, and asked God for strength.

David never forgot that he had begun life as a shepherd boy. He loved to sing songs and play his harp. Many of his songs were to remind people that they could discover God in the everyday things of life. He sang about the stars in the night sky, the rolling hills, the crashing waves and the roaring seas.

David also praised God for his goodness, and he wrote about the things that made him sad or worried. Many of his songs and music, called psalms, were used in the worship of God in the Temple.

David became one of the richest and most powerful rulers ever. He could have whatever he wanted. One day, when his army was away fighting battles, David was gazing out across the rooftops from his palace when he saw a beautiful woman. Although he was married, David wanted to have this woman as his wife, too.

41

David secretly arranged for the woman's husband to be killed in battle. Before long, David married the woman. Her name was Bathsheba.

God knew what David had done, and God was angry. He sent Nathan the prophet, a good and holy man, to confront King David with what he had done wrong.

Nathan continued, "One day an important visitor came to town. The rich man wanted to give him a fine meal. But, rather than kill one of his own sheep for the meal, the rich man took the poor man's only lamb and killed it."

"What!" exploded David. "That's terrible! The man should be punished!"

"Be careful," said Nathan. "God thinks that you are just like that man!"

Nathan told David a story: "Once upon a time," said Nathan, "there was a rich man who had many flocks of sheep..." (Nathan knew that David had been a shepherd and would know all about sheep.)

"In the same town," continued Nathan, "there was a poor man who had only one little lamb. He loved it dearly. He treated it like one of the family." David nodded. He had looked after lambs like that.

Later, David picked up his harp and began to write a song to God.

"Make my heart clean," he wrote. "Help me to do what is right."

He was a good king, and a faithful servant of God, but the wrong he did affected his family for the rest of his life.

David wondered what Nathan meant.

Nathan said, "God made you king, and gave you great riches, but you stole another man's wife, and then you had him killed. You thought nobody knew. But God knew."

David was so sorry, he did not know what to say. Nathan said, "David, you have done bad things, but because you are truly sorry God will forgive you."

Then Nathan added, "But what you have done will bring unhappiness to your family, and that can't be avoided."

43

KING SOLOMON

Right Wrong

King Solomon was famous. He was rich. He lived in a huge palace, and sat on a golden throne. He drank from golden goblets and ate off golden plates.

King Solomon was also wise. When his father David died, Solomon had a dream in which God said, "Ask me for whatever you want."

Solomon replied, "Please give me wisdom to know the difference between right and wrong and to rule kindly and fairly." God was pleased with his answer. He not only promised to give Solomon wisdom but also wealth and a long life.

Solomon's greatest wish was to build a house for God, a Temple, in Jerusalem. He chose the finest stone to build it, and asked the king of Tyre for cedars from Lebanon for the roof and the inside walls.

The whole world heard of Solomon's wisdom, and kings and rulers came from many lands to him to ask for help. But Solomon was also a poet and a scholar, famous for his proverbs and songs. He studied the natural world, and knew all about plants, animals and birds, reptiles and fish. His trading ships brought him animals from other lands.

Soon, ordinary people asked him to settle their quarrels. One day, two desperate women came to Solomon. They lived in the same house. The first woman said, "Please help us, your majesty. We both had new babies, and this woman's baby died in the night while we were asleep. She came and stole my baby, and left me with her dead child."

"No, I didn't," said the second woman. "This is my baby."

"Bring me a sword!" said Solomon. "Cut the baby in half."

"No!" said the first woman. "Give her the baby."

"The king is right!" said the second woman.

Then Solomon knew straight away which woman was the baby's mother. The child was given to the first woman, and the other woman was sent away.

Solomon gave the very best to God to decorate the Temple: gold, silver, bronze and precious stones. And when it was finished, Solomon prayed with all his people, and dedicated the Temple to God. "May the whole world know that you are God," said Solomon.

In a faraway land, the queen of Sheba heard of Solomon's wisdom, his riches, and his dedication to God. She travelled many miles to bring him gifts: gold and spices and precious stones. "Now I have seen all this with my own eyes," she said, "I know that your God is with you."

Solomon became richer and richer. He had fleets of ships and thousands of horses and chariots. He began to forget that he had promised to serve God all his life. He allowed his many foreign wives to worship their own idols and even worshipped them himself. And so God was angry and said to him, "Because you have done this, your descendants will not rule over Israel for ever."

ELIJAH AND THE ANGRY KING

Elijah was a prophet. He was a good and holy man who listened carefully to God and obeyed him. Then he had the important, and difficult, job of telling people what God had said. Often people did not want to know, and sometimes it made them angry.

"I've often heard of people feeding the birds!" chuckled Elijah. "But it's not often I have heard about birds feeding people."

One day, God sent Elijah with a message for the king of Israel. King Ahab was a bad king who worshipped an idol called Baal instead of worshipping God. Many of his people did the same. This made God very sad.

"God says, 'There will be no rain in the land, not even a drop of dew, for at least two years,'" said Elijah.

No one likes giving bad news to a king – they often get angry! King Ahab was very angry when he heard about the drought. Elijah knew he was in great danger, and he needed a good place to hide.

God told him to go far away and live in the wild by a small stream.

God promised Elijah that he would look after him. Elijah could get water from the stream and he promised to send Elijah food. And, as soon as Elijah sat down by the little stream, some ravens flapped over the horizon carrying food in their beaks! They brought him food every morning and every evening.

Time passed, and there was no rain. The brook dried up. The crops did not grow and there wasn't enough flour to make bread. Then God told Elijah to go to a small town where he would be looked after by a widow.

As soon as Elijah reached the town, he saw a widow collecting firewood.

"May I have a drink of water?" asked Elijah, "... and some bread please?"

The poor woman was at her wits' end. "You must be joking!" she cried. "I have almost nothing left – only a handful of flour and a tiny drop of olive oil."

So, Elijah set off to challenge the king to a contest: this would be the way to decide whether to follow Baal, or to follow the true God, the living God.

They met on the top of Mount Carmel.

"I will build an altar to God," said Elijah, "and prepare a sacrifice. You do the same. Then we shall ask our gods to send down fire. The one who answers is the living God."

And so Elijah prepared his altar; and the 450 prophets of Baal did the same.

First the prophets of Baal gathered round the altar to Baal. They called and shouted, "O Baal, send down fire!"

Nothing happened. They shouted louder and louder; they danced themselves into a frenzy. Eventually they gave up, exhausted.

"I am just about to make a last meal for me and my son ... then we will both starve to death!"

"Please don't worry," said Elijah gently. "Go home and bake me a small loaf. God will look after us." God had already promised Elijah that the widow's bowl of flour and her jug of oil would not run out until the rains returned and the drought was ended.

After the woman had made the loaf, the bowl of flour and the jug of oil were full again. The woman could not believe her eyes. And so each day she had enough flour and oil to make bread for herself and her son, and bread for Elijah. God himself was looking after them.

The time came for Elijah to leave the town. God told him to meet King Ahab, and then he would send rain to fall on the land.

Later that day, Elijah was ready.

He dug a trench round God's altar and ordered jars of water to be poured over the sacrifice, so that it ran into the trench.

Then he called upon God. "I am your servant," he prayed. "And now, send down fire and show you are the living God."

Suddenly a bright streak of fire flashed down from heaven, burning up the sacrifice and the altar in seconds.

Everyone fell to their knees in awe. "Elijah's God is the living God," they shouted.

And on that day the first drops of rain fell on the land once more.

JOSIAH THE BOY KING

"Long live the king!' shouted the palace official. The small boy stood unsteadily in robes that were too big for him.

Everyone in the palace doubted whether Josiah would live long at all. His father had been murdered. And his father, like his grandfather before him, had left a trail of bloodshed, sorcery and idol worship across Judah. They had had many bad kings, and few good ones.

Josiah stood in the ruins of the great Temple in Jerusalem where once the true God was worshipped.

He wept as he looked at the dirt and filth, and the images of pagan gods his ancestors had worshipped. "O Lord God," prayed the boy king. "Help me to do what is right. May I serve you in everything I do."

God answered Josiah's prayer. There were still a few good people in Judah who wanted to serve God, and so, when Josiah was a young man,

So Josiah called together all the elders of Jerusalem and read from the Book of the Law.

"I promise to serve God with all my heart for the rest of my life," he said. And all the elders agreed.

The Temple was cleaned up and the idols and their altars were broken up and burned in a huge bonfire.

Throughout Judah the altars on the hills where people had worshipped idols were broken down, and God was worshipped once more.

Then the people celebrated throughout Judah.

"The Book of the Law says we must remember how God rescued his people from slavery in Egypt," said Josiah.

So the people had the biggest and best Passover party for hundreds of years.

he sent a message to the high priest in the Temple.

"Find some good workmen – carpenters, builders and stonemasons – and start to repair the Temple."

A few days later, the high priest came to King Josiah. "Look at this old scroll," he said. "The workmen found it." And he read it aloud.

Josiah started to cry. "It's the Book of the Law," he said. "We've broken God's Law. What shall we do?"

Josiah sent for Huldah the prophetess. "Tell me what to do," he begged.

"God is angry with his people and he is going to bring disaster on Jerusalem," said Huldah.

Josiah and his officials hung their heads. The Temple had been used to worship Baal; some terrible things had happened, and no one had stopped them.

"But because you are sorry, and you want to serve God," continued Huldah, "it will not happen in your lifetime."

Josiah reigned for many years, and for all that time, he worshipped and obeyed God.

But after Josiah's death, the words of Huldah the prophetess came true: the great Babylonian army attacked Judah, destroyed the city of Jerusalem and completely wrecked the Temple.

King Nebuchadnezzar took all the gold and silver treasures from God's Temple and took many captives, making them walk all the way to Babylon to be his slaves.

And so, once more, God's people were taken away into slavery. But even then, God promised that one day he would rescue them.

51

DANIEL AND THE LIONS

Daniel's job was to help King Darius look after his vast empire.

Daniel was so good at his job that one day the king said, "Daniel is so trustworthy and reliable, I will put him in charge of my whole empire!"

For most of his life, Daniel had lived in Babylon. He had been taken there as a captive from the land of Judah. The people of Babylon did not serve God. But Daniel prayed three times a day. He did everything he could to live the way God wanted him to.

When they saw Daniel with the king, the Babylonian leaders who had been helping to rule the empire were not pleased. They were so jealous that they started plotting to kill Daniel.

"But we cannot kill Daniel ourselves," whispered one of them. "We'd get caught."

"I've got an idea!" said another, and he explained his crafty plan.

Daniel's enemies all agreed it was a brilliant idea and the next day they rushed to the palace, and asked for an audience with the king.

"King Darius, may you live for ever!" they said, bowing low. "You are such a wonderful and marvellous king we think everyone should pray only to you!"

The king blushed as the leader continued, "And if anyone is caught praying to anyone else, we think they should be thrown into the lions' den!"

The king agreed, and a new law was made: *For the next thirty days people must pray only to King Darius. Anyone found praying to someone else will be thrown to the lions. Signed, King Darius.*

53

The leaders rubbed their hands with glee and raced to Daniel's house. They knew that Daniel prayed to God three times a day. Often he left his window open, and people could see – and sometimes hear – Daniel talking to God.

As soon as Daniel began to pray, his door burst open and the band of jealous leaders tumbled in.

Within minutes Daniel was dragged in front of King Darius.

"We caught Daniel praying to God when he should have been praying to you!" the leaders exclaimed.

"Well," said the king, who liked Daniel very much, "I'll let him off this time."

King Darius returned to his palace. He did not sleep a wink. He knew he had been tricked. And by now Daniel would be dead...

The following morning King Darius stood by the stone door of the lions' den. He felt very sad. Suddenly, he heard a voice from inside!

"O King, live for ever!" said Daniel. "God sent his angel and the lions haven't touched me."

King Darius was overjoyed and immediately ordered the den to be opened. Daniel was lifted out. There was not a mark on him. God had looked after Daniel.

'You can't!" they replied. "Once made, a law cannot be changed!"

The king was horrified. He summoned his best lawyers and they studied their scrolls. It was true: the law could not be changed. Daniel would have to be thrown to the lions.

With tears in his eyes, King Darius watched Daniel being carried to the den full of hungry lions. A huge stone was placed across the entrance. The king watched as the door was closed. Then, with a very heavy heart, he added his own seal-mark to the stone door. Only Daniel's God could rescue him now.

King Darius turned to his soldiers.

"Go and fetch those evil men who tricked me into putting Daniel into the lions' den," he said.

"And from now on," said the king, "there is a new law. Everyone must love and serve Daniel's God, the true and living God, who has the power to save, even from the mouths of lions."

"The Temple is rebuilt," his brother reported, "but the walls and gates of the city are still broken down, and our enemies keep stopping us from rebuilding."

When his brother had gone, Nehemiah prayed, "Lord God, what should I do?"

Nehemiah and his brother walked in the gardens of the royal palace at Susa in Babylon.

Like all the Israelites living in Babylon, Nehemiah longed to hear good news about Jerusalem.

Nehemiah was sad. What could he do – so many miles away from God's city?

When he held out the wine cup for King Artaxerxes of Persia the next day, the king asked, "What's the matter?"

When he got to Jerusalem, what a sight met his eyes! The many gates of the city had been burned down, and the walls were just heaps of rubble. The Temple stood up on the hill, strong and majestic, but the city walls could have let an army through.

Nehemiah was terrified: servants weren't supposed to show their feelings. But he prayed to God quickly, and decided to tell the king how much he longed to visit Jerusalem.

The king listened carefully, for Nehemiah was a completely trustworthy servant.

Nehemiah could hardly believe his ears when the king said, "You must go back home to Jerusalem. Go with my blessing, and have some cedar wood from my forests for the repairs."

Before long Nehemiah set off for Jerusalem.

Nehemiah had not told anyone the reason for his visit, but later he went out after dark for a secret inspection of the walls and gates, taking only a few trusted friends with him.

The next day, Nehemiah called together all the city leaders.

"We're in trouble," he said. "Anyone could attack Jerusalem, and our enemies are laughing at us. We must get to work straight away."

Everyone worked together, thanking God for Nehemiah. But before long, the enemies of God's people came to sneer and laugh, "If even a fox walked on those walls, they would fall down," they shouted.

In a few months, God's people were settled back in Jerusalem, and Nehemiah called them all together into the square. Ezra the scribe read from the Book of the Law, and everyone there – men, women and children – bowed down and worshipped God.

When the people realised how good and holy God was, they began to cry. But Nehemiah told them, "Today is a day for celebration. Go and enjoy yourselves."

The people of Israel had not had such a good time since the days of Joshua.

Nehemiah encouraged the people to carry on, but soon they got tired. They were afraid of being attacked.

"Remember," said Nehemiah, "God is with us, and he is bigger and stronger than any of our enemies."

The enemies would not go away, so Nehemiah prayed and then he took action.

He made sure the builders always had their swords with them, and half the group stood guard while the others worked. That frightened off the enemies.

The men worked from dawn until dusk, and even when they stopped to eat or drink, they did not put their swords down.

And so the walls got higher and higher, and the gates were made secure. In fifty-two days the work was finished!

Later that month, the people met together and promised to serve God all their lives.

The musicians and singers walked round the walls, dedicating Jerusalem once more to God, and the whole city was full of happy people, praising God.

Nehemiah's faith in God never wavered, and he was a strong leader. But sometimes he wondered, what would happen to God's people?

At that time, God also spoke through the prophet Malachi: God would send a Saviour, "Messiah", God's chosen one.

THE FIRST CHRISTMAS

Mary and Joseph travelled many, many miles to get from their home in Nazareth to Bethlehem. Mary was tired because she was expecting a baby.

When they reached the town it was full of visitors and there was nowhere for them to stay.

At last they found a kindly innkeeper who agreed to let Mary and Joseph sleep in the stable beside his inn. "It's the best I can do," he said. "It's a bit draughty, but at least it's dry."

"Thank you," sighed Mary.

That night Mary's baby was born. She wrapped him in strips of cloth and made a bed for him in a manger.

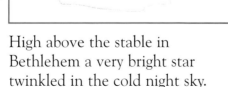

Mary and Joseph looked at the new baby lying in the straw-filled manger. They knew he was very special. God had sent his angel to tell them both that the baby would be called Jesus – which means Saviour.

High above the stable in Bethlehem a very bright star twinkled in the cold night sky.

On a hillside near the town some shepherds who were looking after their sheep were about to get a terrible shock.

Suddenly the sky was filled with a dazzling bright light, and an angel said, "Don't be afraid! This is wonderful news for all the world. Tonight a baby has been born in Bethlehem. He is God's own Son, and he will bring peace and joy to all people!"

Millions of angels filled the sky, singing praises to God.

The shepherds could hardly believe their ears and eyes, but when the angels had gone they leapt to their feet and ran down the hillside. They found the baby Jesus with Mary and Joseph in the stable. It was just as the angel had said.

Far away, some wise men who studied the stars saw the bright star at the time Jesus was born. They knew it was a special sign of a king's birth. So they set off, following the star, until they arrived in Jerusalem. There they decided to visit the palace.

The wise men continued with their search until eventually they found Mary and Joseph and the child Jesus in Bethlehem. They had brought special gifts with them, and so they gave gold, frankincense and myrrh to this very special baby.

"You have a very wonderful child," they whispered to Mary. "He will be the most important person the world has ever known!"

Later, an angel told the wise men: "Don't tell Herod you have found the new king." So they left the country secretly.

"Where is the new king?" they asked King Herod. "We have come to see him."

Herod was worried by this news. He was also annoyed. Another king? A rival!

"Keep searching," advised Herod. "When you have found him, let me know. I would like to meet this new king, too." But secretly, Herod planned to find and destroy the baby king.

Mary held her son tightly as she thought about the things the wise men said. What did they mean?

King Herod was furious when he realised the wise men had not come back. He planned to murder all the boy babies in the country.

Mary and Joseph packed up their things and took Jesus to Egypt for safety. It was some time before they could return home to Nazareth.

JESUS' SPECIAL MESSENGER

Before Jesus was born, God planned to send a messenger to tell the world about him. That messenger was John, the son of Elizabeth and Zechariah.

For many years, they had prayed for a child of their own. But now Elizabeth was old, there seemed to be no hope.

But then something amazing happened! Zechariah was in the Temple, doing his work as a priest, when an angel appeared and told him that he and Elizabeth would have a child. They must call him John, and he would grow up to be God's messenger.

The old priest could not believe what the angel said, and from that moment he could not speak.

When John grew up, he spent time alone in the desert, thinking and praying. He knew that God had chosen him to be a special messenger, to tell people that God had sent his Son to live among them.

John's message was simple: "Stop doing bad things, and do things which please God. God's promised Saviour is coming soon." He baptised people in the River Jordan as a sign of the new life which only God can give.

One day, Jesus came to the river and asked to be baptised. "But I ought to be baptised by you!" John said. He did as Jesus asked, and suddenly the sky opened, and people heard God's voice saying, "You are my Son. I am very pleased with you."

But sure enough, Elizabeth was expecting a baby! At the same time, she found out that her cousin, Mary, was pregnant too. Mary's child would be called Jesus, and he was the promised Saviour, God's own Son. When the two women met, they were so excited that even Elizabeth's baby jumped for joy inside her!

When Elizabeth's baby was born, she called him John, as the angel had told her. Some of the family were surprised. They thought the baby should be called Zechariah, like his father. But Zechariah, who still could not speak, wrote down the name "John" for everyone to see. And at that moment, Zechariah was able to speak once more.

John watched as Jesus walked away. Now Jesus was ready to begin his very special work in the world. And John had helped Jesus begin, by getting the people ready.

He carried on telling people, "Make room for God in your life! Be baptised, as a sign that you want to live God's way."

From the time Jesus started teaching the people about God, John's life was in danger. King Herod did not like the message John was preaching, so he put John in prison, and later had him executed.

When Jesus heard about John's death, he was very sad.

Everybody was talking about him – Jesus from Nazareth who healed people, and taught them about a new way of life in God's kingdom.

"He's like John the Baptist," said one, "he's powerful, a bit frightening…"

"He's kind," said another. "He talks about God's love – and some of his stories are really funny…"

Down by Lake Galilee, two fishermen were sitting mending their nets. Just then Jesus came along.

"Is this your boat?" he asked. And almost before they knew what was happening, Peter and Andrew were out on the lake with Jesus in the boat. Jesus talked to the crowd that had gathered on the shore.

"Don't be scared," said Jesus. "Come with me – we have work to do. From now on, you'll be fishing for people, catching them for God's kingdom."

So the four fishermen pulled their boats up on the shore, and went with Jesus.

Crowds of people followed Jesus everywhere he went. They wanted to hear about God's kingdom.

But some people did not like what Jesus was doing. The Pharisees and the teachers of the law were very religious, but they did not think Jesus was doing God's work. They decided to watch him carefully.

One day, four men brought their friend to Jesus to be healed. He could not walk, so they carried him on a stretcher.

When they got to the house where Jesus was, they could not get in because of all the people there. One of them had a bright idea. They carried their friend up to the roof of the house – and began to dig.

Jesus just looked
...eter. And Peter
... what Jesus said.
"Quick!" shouted
... "It's a miracle!"
...denly, the nets were so
... of wriggling fish that they
were bursting.

Peter and Andrew started to
pull in the nets, while shouting to
their friends, James and John, to come
and help them.

When the fishermen saw all the
fish, they were completely amazed.
They looked at Jesus, and they felt
almost frightened.

When Jesus had finished speaking he said to Peter, "Take the
boat out into the deeper water and put down your nets."

"Master," said Peter, "we fished all night and didn't catch a
thing. We don't fish during the day."

So Jesus said to them, "Is it easier to
heal this man or to forgive his
sins?" And he turned back to the
man and said, "Get up and walk."

The man got up and walked.

All the people watching were
thrilled, and a bit frightened, but
they thanked God, saying, "What
wonderful things we have seen
today!"

The religious leaders watched in
silence.

The roof was only made of
wood, brushwood and
mud, so they made quick
work of it.

The four friends
let the man
down through the hole, until he was lying in front
of Jesus.

"Your sins are forgiven," said Jesus.
The religious leaders were furious. "What does he
mean?" they said. "Only God can forgive sins."

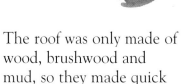

Matthew held a big party for Jesus and invited his friends, including a number of tax collectors. They all had a great time – lots of good food and the best wine.

When the religious leaders found out what was going on, they asked some of Jesus' followers, "Why do you bother with that sort of person? They're not worth it."

Jesus heard the religious leaders complaining, so he came across to talk to them.

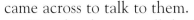

A few days later, Jesus was walking by Lake Galilee when he saw a tax collector called Matthew. Most ordinary people disliked tax collectors – they worked for the Romans, and often they overcharged, keeping the extra money for themselves.

"Come with me," Jesus said, so Matthew left his tax collecting and became one of Jesus' followers.

"People who are well don't need a doctor, but people who are ill do," he said. "My message of God's kingdom isn't for people who think they are good – it's for people who know they are bad, and need God's help."

Jesus taught people about God's kingdom.

"It's like this," said Jesus. "The people who are truly happy are those who know they need God.

"If you love and obey God, then you are like a light on a hill, guiding other people to safety."

People were sometimes puzzled by what Jesus said. Everything seemed upside down in God's kingdom.

Jesus said, "Do not try to get your own back on someone who has done something bad to you: love your enemies, and pray for people who don't like you."

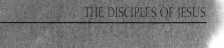

A little while after this, Jesus went up into the hills of Galilee to pray.

He spent the whole night praying, and when he came down, he had chosen twelve special friends out of his many followers to be his disciples and learn from him.

These twelve friends would spend the next three years with Jesus, learning about God, seeing what Jesus did, and doing the work he gave them to do.

They were Peter, Andrew, James, John, Matthew, Philip, Bartholomew, Thomas, James, Simon, Judas and Judas Iscariot.

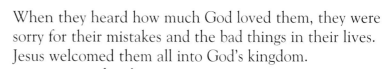

When they heard how much God loved them, they were sorry for their mistakes and the bad things in their lives. Jesus welcomed them all into God's kingdom.

"When you pray," said Jesus, "talk to God, your Father in heaven, and ask him for everything you need – even though he already knows.

"Just look at the birds in the sky – and the wild flowers. They don't worry – God gives them food and clothing. What's important is to live your life to please God."

And so, each day, more and more people became followers of Jesus.

69

Jesus was a great story-teller. He used to gather the crowd round him, and paint a picture in words.

"Now," said Jesus, "it's not enough just to listen to what I say about living God's way. You have to put it into practice – otherwise you will be like the second man in my story.

"There was once a man who decided to build a house. He thought carefully first, and then he dug the foundations deep into the rock.

"It was hard work, but, when it was finished, it was solid and well built, and so the man moved into the house with his family.

"The next night, the thunder crashed, the lightning flashed, the wind blew and the rain fell down in torrents.

"A stream of water rushed past the man's house, but because it was built on rock, it stood firm and dry.

"But there was another man who built a house. He didn't really care about foundations, and he quickly put up a house on sand, any-old-how.

"It was finished in no time at all.

"The next night, the thunder crashed, the lightning flashed, the wind blew and the rain fell down in torrents.

"A stream of water rushed straight at the man's house, and washed the sand underneath it clean away.

"When the family woke up the next morning, all was calm and peaceful. The house was safe because it had solid foundations.

   "That house stood there for many, many years.

"With a bang and a crash, the house which was built on sand with no foundations collapsed, and the man and his family had nowhere to live.

"Now," said Jesus, "the first man is my true follower. He listens to what I say – and he does it. But the second man is like someone who hears what I say – even agrees with it – but does not put it into practice. He is like the man who built his house on sand – and everything was washed away."

A PARTY FOR JESUS

One evening Jesus went to have supper with an important man called Simon. The day had been long, hot and dusty, and Jesus was pleased to have somewhere to rest and recover.

"Come in, come in," said Simon. "I'm longing to talk to you."

In Jesus' time, the servants usually washed the guests' feet for them. But Simon was so excited by Jesus' visit that he rushed Jesus to the table and started bombarding him with questions.

72

Soon the news spread that Jesus was in the town. People gathered around the doors and windows of Simon's house. They were trying to catch a glimpse of Jesus or, even better, to hear what he was discussing with Simon.

As the crowd peeped around the door and peered through the windows, a young woman crept through the crowd and came into Simon's house.

There were tears in her eyes as she stood behind Jesus. Without saying a word she took a jar of very precious and expensive perfume from under her cloak and began to pour it on Jesus' feet.

She had made many mistakes in her life, and had done bad things. But now she wanted to say sorry.

By now she was crying so much that her tears were falling on Jesus' feet. She tried to wipe them away with her long hair.

73

Simon was shocked.
"Go away," he said to the woman. "We don't want people like you here!" He was thinking, "If Jesus knew what sort of person she was, he wouldn't go anywhere near her."

But Jesus turned to Simon and his friends. With a twinkle in his eye he began to tell them a story.

"Listen!" he said. "Once there were two people, both in debt to the same money-lender. One owed five hundred silver coins and the other fifty."

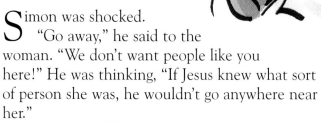

Jesus smiled and asked, "Which of the two people who owed the money would love the money-lender the most?" he asked.

"Easy!" Simon replied. "The one who owed the most."

"When I came to your house, Simon," said Jesus, "I was hot and my feet were dusty. You didn't even offer me the chance to wash.

"This woman has bathed my feet with perfume and tears. She is sorry for all the wrong things she has done, and she knows that God has forgiven her. Now she is showing how much she loves me."

The people listening to Jesus knew that money-lenders were greedy people. So the two people Jesus was talking about were in deep trouble.

"Well," continued Jesus, "neither of them could pay back what they owed, and the money-lender let them both off! He cancelled their debts!"

The listeners around the table gasped. What money-lender would ever do such a thing?

Jesus looked at the young woman.

"Go on your way," he said to her, gently. "You are a new person."

The woman left the house much happier than when she had come in. Jesus had given her a new start in life. She would never be the same again.

Simon blushed as he realised that Jesus was right.

THE HIDDEN TREASURE

People loved listening to the stories Jesus told. The tales were sometimes funny, but always had a hidden meaning, which made people stop and think.

One day a crowd of people gathered around Jesus to hear another story.

"Let me tell you how important it is to love God, and to be in his kingdom," said Jesus. "It's a bit like this...

"One day a man was crossing a field when he stumbled over something sticking out of the ground.

"The man yelled as he stubbed his toe, and was just about to limp away when he spied something glinting in the sunlight.

"He knelt down and scraped away at the soil. He had not tripped over a rock, but an old wooden box. What was more, he'd kicked the box open, and inside he could see gold!

"The man leapt in the air, and yelled and cheered," said Jesus. "And he ran home faster than he had ever done in his life (even though he had stubbed his toe).

"He knew what he had to do – sell everything he owned to buy the field. That was the only thing that mattered.

"He dashed into his house and grabbed all the pots and pans he could find. He was so single minded he didn't say anything to his wife. She thought he had gone mad.

"Then the man rushed to the box where his wife kept her few trinkets of jewellery. She was very worried now. He scraped together every coin he could find, and then gathered blankets, rugs and furniture.

"The man stacked everything they possessed on the back of his donkey, intending to sell the lot, including the donkey. Then he explained to his wife what he was up to.

"Waving goodbye, he set off for market. Before long, he had sold everything except for the clothes he stood up in.

"The man held his bulging money-bag carefully and raced off to find the owner of the field. Soon he was banging at his door.

"The owner was surprised, but he didn't refuse the money, and before long, the man and his wife were rich beyond their wildest dreams.

"They had given up everything they had in order to own that treasure. It was a risk, but it was worth it. That's like being part of God's kingdom," said Jesus.

"It's worth giving up everything to find it!"

77

THE STORM ON THE LAKE

By the shore of Lake Galilee there was a huge crowd of people. All day long they had been listening to Jesus as he told them stories about the kingdom of God. Jesus healed the people who were ill and he answered question after question from people in the crowd.

"What's heaven like?"

"How can I get there?"

"Will you come and heal my mum?"

The crowds pushed closer to Jesus, eager to hear one of his stories, or hear more about God's kingdom. They were fascinated by this man from Galilee. There was definitely something different – and special – about him.

Sometimes Jesus' disciples got tired of all the crowds, but Jesus was always patient, always kind.

"I wish I could tell them all to go away!" Peter muttered under his breath. Jesus heard him, and shook his head, with just a twinkle in his eye.

At the end of the day, Jesus said to his friends, "Let's sail across the lake."

Before long the boat was making its way across Lake Galilee. No one was surprised when Jesus fell asleep.

The sun was setting as the boat sailed out from the shore into open water.

"Jesus must be exhausted," said Peter, steering the boat and glancing at Jesus asleep in the stern.

He didn't like the look of the dark clouds ahead. Lake Galilee was renowned for sudden storms, and there was one coming their way – now!

Hurriedly the men struggled to lower the sail as the wind rapidly rose. The wet canvas slapped wildly in the wind as they tried to make the boat safe.

Soon the waves were crashing about them and the boat was tipping wildly from side to side. "We're all going to drown!" shouted John.

As they clung on to the boat, they suddenly noticed Jesus. He was still fast asleep!

"Quick... wake him!" they all shouted. Andrew staggered to the back of the boat and shook Jesus awake.

"Teacher!" he shouted. "Don't you care that we're all going to drown?"

"Be quiet!" yelled Peter. But even he, an experienced fisherman who had seen many storms in his time, knew that this was a really bad one. They were in danger of capsizing any moment. There would be no hope of rescue in this storm.

The waves were foaming over the bow of the fishing boat now, and the wind was screaming through the rigging. It wouldn't be long before the boat filled with water and they would all drown.

"Who is this man?" Peter asked the others. "Even the wind and waves obey him!"

Jesus stood up. In a very powerful and loud voice, he told the wind, "Be quiet!" Then he turned to the waves and shouted, "Be still!"

Jesus' friends could not believe their eyes. Within seconds the wind dropped and the waves died down. Soon the lake was calm, and there was no sign of a storm.

Then Jesus turned to his friends. "Why are you so afraid? Have you still no faith?" he asked.

The men just did not know what to make of it all. They stared at Jesus, amazed.

81

JAIRUS'S DAUGHTER

Peter leapt ashore as the boat landed at Capernaum. When Jesus and his friends got out, they saw a crowd of people, waiting for Jesus. And pushing to the front of that crowd was a desperate man, Jairus the synagogue ruler. Jairus threw himself onto the ground in front of Jesus.

"Please, help me!" he sobbed. "It's my daughter, she's very ill. Please come to my house. I'm afraid she's dying."

Jesus helped the man up, and began to follow him through the crowd.

In the crowd was a desperate woman. She had had a secret illness for twelve years which no one could cure, but she was sure that Jesus could make her better. She pushed through the people around Jesus, and touched his cloak. The moment she touched his cloak, the illness went.

"Who touched me?" asked Jesus.

Nobody answered.

"It's this crowd," said Peter. "They're all around you."

Just then, a messenger came from Jairus's house.

"Your daughter is dead," he said. "Don't bother Jesus any more."

Jairus covered his face and sobbed, but Jesus said to him, "Don't be afraid. Only believe, and your daughter will be well."

"Someone touched me," said Jesus. "I felt the power go out of me."

The woman was scared. She fell on the ground at Jesus' feet. Quickly she told him what she had done, and why.

"Your faith has cured you," said Jesus. "Don't worry. Go in peace."

Jesus took the girl's hand, and said, "Little girl, get up!"

Immediately the girl got up.

"Give her something to eat," said Jesus. "She's hungry."

The girl's parents were completely amazed, but Jesus told them not to tell anyone.

When they arrived at the house, another crowd of people was weeping and wailing.

Jesus went into the room with Peter, James and John, and the girl's parents.

"Stop wailing," he said to the mourners. "She isn't dead, she's sleeping."

They all laughed at Jesus, because they knew she was dead.

83

THE AMAZING PICNIC

Everyone was excited. The news spread like wildfire.

"Haven't you heard? Jesus is coming to Galilee!"

The boy grabbed five small rolls and two dried fish for his lunch, and ran down to the shore of Lake Galilee to see if he could find Jesus.

A huge crowd of people was gathering by the edge of the lake. The boy could see old people, young men and women, boys and girls. Some were hobbling on sticks and others who couldn't see were being helped along.

The boy ran to see Jesus climbing out of a small fishing boat. He watched as Jesus walked around talking to people, listening to them, making the sick ones well again.

Then Jesus began speaking to the huge crowd. His special friends, the disciples, were with him.

The boy sat down to listen. Jesus told some marvellous stories. Soon the sun was setting. The boy stretched and rubbed his eyes. "Have I really been here all day?" he said to himself.

Jesus had stopped talking now. But one of his friends shouted to the crowd, "It's time for you to go home now!" he said. "Go home and have something to eat!"

But no one wanted to go. They wanted to hear more about God and his kingdom. They just sat there.

The boy was looking at the food he had brought with him – five barley rolls and two small dried fish.

The boy thrust his small basket of food into the hands of a startled disciple.

"Thank you," the disciple said. He turned to Jesus and showed him the food, muttering, "This won't go very far."

Jesus took the food and said, "Thank you," to God. He took one of the rolls and broke it, and gave it to his disciples to share out.

Jesus turned to Philip, one of his disciples, and asked, "Where are we going to get food for all these people?"

Philip was dumbstruck. "We can't feed all these people!" he stammered. "For a start, we're miles from the nearest town, and anyway, it would cost a fortune."

The other disciples agreed with Peter. "Tell them to go home," they said.

But just at that moment, one of Jesus' disciples noticed a boy sitting on a rock…

Suddenly there was plenty for everyone. Something amazing had happened!

When everyone had finished eating, the disciples cleared up – there were twelve baskets full of leftovers. As the boy walked home, he knew it was the biggest, most amazing picnic ever!

THE LOST SHEEP

Everyone in Israel knew something about sheep – they were everywhere!

And everyone knew that sheep needed a shepherd to look after them.

Sometimes the shepherd had to protect his flock from wild dogs or even bears.

And at night he herded them into the sheepfold, with himself as the gate.

So, it was not surprising that one of Jesus' stories was all about a lost sheep.

"Once," said Jesus, "there was a shepherd. He had a hundred sheep, and he knew each of them by name.

"One day, he counted them all, to make sure they were all there.

"But, however hard he counted, he could count only ninety-nine sheep, no more and no less. One was missing.

"The shepherd was delighted. He gently untangled its fleece from the thorn-bush, and carried it back to the flock on his shoulders.

"Suddenly he heard a distant bleat. He ran over rocks, clambered through brambles, paddled through puddles and staggered after the sound.

"There in a thornbush was his lost sheep, all tangled up.

"He searched high and low. He looked and he listened. He called and he whistled. No sheep.

"As soon as he got home, the shepherd called all his friends and neighbours together.

" 'I've found my lost sheep!' he said. 'Let's have a party.'

"God's like that shepherd," said Jesus. "He's always looking for people who have strayed away from him. He searches high and low; he looks and he listens; he calls and he whistles.

"He never stops searching until he finds them and brings them safely home."

"So the shepherd set off to find his missing sheep.

THE GOOD SAMARITAN

People enjoyed asking Jesus questions, especially as he often answered them by telling a story.

One day a man asked Jesus, "How can I please God and be his friend for ever?"

Jesus smiled. "Keep God's rules. Live the way God wants you to," he said. "Love God first, then love your neighbour as you love yourself."

The man who asked the question thought he would then trick Jesus. "But who is my neighbour?" he asked.

With a twinkle in his eye Jesus began to tell a story. Everyone listening fell silent.

"One day a man had to make the journey from Jerusalem to Jericho. Now, that road was dusty and dirty and no one liked to travel along it, especially on their own, because of the robbers.

"Well, sure enough, the man was attacked by robbers who beat him so badly that they left him for dead.

"Soon after, a holy man came along that lonely road. He'd help the man, wouldn't he? But when he spotted the injured man, he passed by on the other side of the road. He didn't want to get his hands dirty.

"Some time later another holy man reached the place where the man lay. He pretended not to see, and passed by on the other side of the road, too. Things were looking very bad indeed for the poor man.

"Then the Samaritan lifted the man on to his donkey and took him to the nearest inn.

"He told the innkeeper to care for the injured man and gave him two silver coins to pay for everything, promising to pay for anything else the wounded man needed.

"Finally a man from Samaria came along. Now Samaritans were not very popular. People said unkind things about them, and the religious leaders told people to have nothing to do with them.

"This Samaritan stopped and, even though he was supposed to be an enemy of the wounded man, he knelt down to help him. He saw to his wounds, and carefully bandaged him up.

The man could only give one answer. "The one who helped him," he said.

"That's the way God wants you to live," said Jesus.

When Jesus had finished his story the people shifted uncomfortably. Jesus looked at the man who had asked the question.

"Who do you think acted like a neighbour to the man attacked by the robbers?" he asked.

93

THE LOVING FATHER

One day Jesus told a story about a rich farmer who had two sons.

"The elder son worked from dawn till dusk every day on his father's farm.

"But the younger son did not like hard work, so he asked his father to give him his share of the land that would come to him when his father died. Then he sold his share and left home with all the money.

"When the father saw his son staggering over the hill, he rushed to meet him.

"The son was about to say sorry for running away and wasting his father's money, when his father hugged him, and gave him a fine new robe and a gold ring to wear.

" 'I don't deserve this,' said the young man in disbelief.

" 'I forgive you,' replied his father. Then he held a huge party.

94

In a faraway land the young man spent his money on parties and fine clothes. Because he was rich, he was very popular.

"But when the money ran out, so did his friends. Before long he had nothing. And when a famine hit the country, he had nothing to eat.

"He ended up in rags, and the only job he could get was looking after some pigs. He was so hungry he felt like eating the pigs' food!

"The young man was sad – all he could do was go back to his father, say he was sorry and ask for a job on the farm. So he started the long trudge home.

The elder brother was cross – after all, he had worked hard, and had never given his father any trouble.

"His father told him, 'But this is my son who was lost, and is found! I thought he was dead, but instead he's alive!'"

When Jesus finished his story he said, "That story gives you a good idea of what God is like. He's like a loving father who is always ready to forgive. When you come back to him to say sorry for the wrong things you have done, he holds a party. That's just the sort of 'dad' God is."

95

JESUS AND THE BLIND MAN

For many years a blind man called Bartimaeus had sat begging by the city gates. He was well used to crowds coming and going, and his keen ears picked up lots of tittle-tattle. For the last few days there had been little talk of anyone but Jesus. Everyone wanted to meet him, including Bartimaeus.

Jesus was on his way to Jerusalem, and as he passed through the city of Jericho, a large crowd followed him.

The crowd moved towards the gates where Bartimaeus sat in the dust and dirt. People were laughing and chattering, pushing and jostling. Bartimaeus knew this was a very special crowd, because Jesus was somewhere in the middle of it!

Bartimaeus took a deep breath then yelled at the top of his voice, "Jesus, Son of David! Take pity on me!"

By now the crowd of people was almost crushing Bartimaeus.

"Be quiet, you silly old fool!" scolded someone.

"Jesus won't be interested in a beggar like you!"

But Bartimaeus took another huge breath and bellowed as loudly as he possibly could, "Son of David! Have pity on me!"

97

People kept telling Bartimaeus to keep quiet, but he shouted so loudly that Jesus heard him above the noise of the crowd.

"Jesus, have pity on me!" he yelled.

"Who's calling me?" asked Jesus.

"It's only a blind beggar," said someone near Jesus. "Take no notice. He's always trying to get someone's attention."

"Bring him to me," said Jesus.

A couple of helpers squeezed through the crowd.

"Hey, Jesus wants to see you!" they sa

In a moment Bartimaeus was standing right in front of Jesus.

The people in the crowd could not believe their eyes.

Jesus smiled, patted Bartimaeus on the shoulder, and together they walked off down the road.

The crowd followe them. Everyone wa amazed at what ha happened. They couldn't stop talki about it.

98

"How can I help you?" asked Jesus, kindly.

"I want to see again," said Bartimaeus.

Jesus looked straight at Bartimaeus. "Go," he said in a clear voice. "Your faith has made you well."

Bartimaeus blinked. The crowd blinked. Suddenly Bartimaeus could see!

Bartimaeus had been sitting begging by the city gates for so many years that no one could believe that he could now see – and walk, leap and jump!

"I really didn't think Jesus would be interested in Bartimaeus," said an old man at the back of the crowd.

"Jesus is interested in everyone," said a little boy nearby. But no one seemed to be listening!

THE MAN IN THE TREE

People in Jericho just couldn't stop talking about Jesus. "Did you hear? The blind beggar can see. Jesus can do miracles! He's coming this way now!"

And so a crowd gathered, waiting to see Jesus.

One of the people trying to see Jesus was a rich man called Zacchaeus, the chief tax collector.

But Zacchaeus was not very tall. He couldn't see over the heads of the crowd, and he couldn't see through the crowd. And because Zacchaeus worked for the Romans, and was known to cheat people, no one would let him through.

The next moment, Jesus stopped and looked up at him. Zacchaeus nearly fell out of the tree in shock.

"Come down, Zacchaeus," said Jesus. "I'm coming to your house today."

Delighted, Zacchaeus leaped down from the tree and led the way to his house.

The people in the crowd were disapproving. What did Jesus want with a bad person like Zacchaeus?

In desperation, Zacchaeus ran ahead of the crowd, and scrambled up a sycomore fig tree. It was not a dignified act.

"He's coming! He's coming!" shouted the crowd, and Zacchaeus leaned forward for a good view.

For Zacchaeus, meeting Jesus was quite an experience. Suddenly, he saw things differently. He was so happy!

He turned to Jesus and said, "Master, I'm giving half my possessions to help poor people, here and now. And I promise to pay back to anyone I have cheated four times the amount of money."

Nobody could quite believe how much Zacchaeus's life had changed – for the better.

"This is the start of your new life with God," said Jesus. "It's what I came to do – to find the people who have strayed away, and put them on the right path in God's kingdom."

JESUS THE KING

The road to Jerusalem was dusty and the disciples were tired.

A few miles from the city Jesus said to two of them, "In the village over there you will find a young donkey which has never been ridden. Untie it and bring it here. And if anyone asks you what you are doing, say, 'The Master needs it.'"

The disciples were surprised, and a bit puzzled. How could Jesus know this? But they did what they were told. They went to the village, found the young donkey and brought it to Jesus.

Meanwhile, some people in Jerusalem were very excited. They had heard that Jesus was on his way! They felt sure he was going to perform some wonderful miracles. He might even chase the Roman army away – they were fed up with being ruled by soldiers from another country.

"Jesus is coming, Jesus is coming!" shouted a little girl.

Everyone rushed to look. They could see him in the distance, riding a young donkey. His friends followed him on foot. They were moving steadily towards the city gates. Some of the people grabbed palm branches to wave at him.

As Jesus came into the city of Jerusalem, people began to wave their palm branches.

103

What sort of king was he? Most kings rode in triumph on warhorses, in rich clothes, with soldiers and servants. Jesus rode humbly into Jerusalem, a king on a donkey.

Other people took off their cloaks and laid them on the ground. The people shouted, they cheered, they clapped their hands.

Years before, the prophets had spoken of a king entering the city, riding a donkey.

"Jesus is our King! God bless the King!" they yelled.

"This place should be a place of prayer!" said Jesus. "But you are cheating the poor. You have turned God's house into a den of thieves!"

Jesus was so angry with the traders that he tipped some of the tables over.

Once inside the city, Jesus went into the Temple courtyard. He looked around him in dismay. The place was full of stalls selling birds and small animals as offerings for the Passover festival.

There were food counters and tables piled high with bags of Temple money. The money-changers often cheated poor people who had to change their ordinary money for Temple money.

From that time the religious leaders tried to find a way to catch Jesus out. His enemies wanted to get rid of him.

THE LAST SUPPER

"What will you give me if I tell you where to find Jesus?" whispered Judas Iscariot.

Judas took the thirty silver coins and walked through the busy streets of the great city. He had betrayed Jesus to his enemies.

Tonight Jesus and his twelve friends were meeting in an upper room to share the special Passover meal.

Jesus' mood was serious. As they sat down to eat, he said, "One of you here will betray me."

Jesus and his friends went to the Garden of Gethsemane. Jesus took Peter, James and John deeper into the trees to pray.

"My Father," he prayed. "Save me from the pain and suffering to come. But I want to do whatever you want."

Suddenly there was a crowd of people, carrying weapons, and torches, led by Judas.

"Master," he said, and kissed Jesus. That was the sign the crowd was waiting for. They seized Jesus and took him away for trial.

All Jesus' friends ran away.

Jesus was taken to the house of Caiaphas, the high priest. Peter and John followed in the shadows.

As Peter sat in the courtyard, wondering what was happening, a servant asked him, "Aren't you one of Jesus' friends?"

"No, I'm not," he replied.

On two other occasions, people asked him if he knew Jesus.

"I do not know him!" shouted Peter.

Just then he heard the cock crow.

He looked across at Judas. Judas got up and left the room.

During the meal, Jesus shared the bread with his friends. "This is my body, given for you," he said.

Then he passed around the special cup of wine. He gave thanks to God and said, "This is my blood, a sign that God will save you."

His friends did not know what he meant.

After the meal, the friends went out of the city into the cool of the Mount of Olives.

"All of you will run away and leave me tonight," said Jesus.

"Not me! I won't," said Peter.

"Before the cock crows tomorrow morning, you will say three times that you don't know me," replied Jesus.

Inside the high priest's house, Caiaphas was angry. No one could produce evidence to sentence Jesus to death. No one could say what Jesus had done wrong.

In all this panic and anger, Jesus stood alone, dignified and silent.

Caiaphas sent Jesus to Pilate, the Roman governor of Jerusalem. He alone had the power to pass the death sentence.

Pilate didn't want to deal with this case. What had the man done wrong? Jesus fascinated him.

"Are you the king of the Jews?" he asked.

"You said so," replied Jesus.

Outside the crowds were shouting. Pilate was afraid there was going to be a riot. He went out and said to the crowd, "It's my custom to release a prisoner at the Passover. Do you want Barabbas the murderer or Jesus of Nazareth?"

"Barabbas!" they shouted. "Crucify Jesus!"

THE EASTER STORY

The morning was cold and dark. The crowds in Jerusalem and certain religious leaders had called for Jesus to be killed, and so he had been sentenced to death although he had done nothing wrong.

The soldiers hit him and called him names. They pushed a crown of thorns upon his head and sent him to the hill called "Golgotha", where criminals were executed.

Jesus was so weak he could not carry the heavy beam of wood, so the soldiers made another man carry it for him.

When they reached the top of the hill, Jesus was nailed to the cross, and it was hoisted up. The sky turned inky black, and thunder rumbled in the distance.

A message was pinned above the cross. It said "Jesus – the King of the Jews".

Two robbers were on crosses either side of Jesus. They were in great pain too. One of them mocked Jesus. "If you're really God's Son, then save us!" he said.

"We're bad, we deserve this," said the other robber. "Jesus has done nothing bad, only good."

Jesus turned to this robber and said, "Today, you will be with me in paradise."

As he was dying Jesus looked down at his mother Mary, standing at the foot of the cross. He asked John, one of his closest friends, to look after her.

The darkness became deeper and then, with a loud cry, Jesus died.

As Jesus died, the sky went pitch black and the earth shook. From inside the Temple there was a dreadful tearing sound as the huge curtain which led to the Most Holy Place ripped in half.

The Roman soldiers gambling for Jesus' clothes were frightened by the earthquake.

One of them whispered to himself, "Truly, this man was the Son of God."

Jesus' body was taken down from the cross, wrapped in a sheet and taken to a tomb in a nearby garden. His friends were so sad. How could this have happened? With great sorrow, they rolled the big stone across the opening.

Two days after Jesus died, very early in the morning, Mary Magdalene went back to the garden to visit the tomb, carrying herbs and special ointments to anoint Jesus' body.

When she reached the tomb, she could not believe her eyes. The stone had been rolled away! Jesus had gone!

Night was falling and the lights of Jerusalem twinkled in the darkness. Mary Magdalene and the other women who were friends of Jesus walked back sadly to the city. They could hardly believe that Jesus was dead.

Suddenly she saw him.

"Master!" she cried.

"Mary," said Jesus. "Go and tell the others you have seen me."

"Jesus is alive again!" shouted Mary as she rushed off to tell everyone the good news. "Jesus is alive!"

JESUS IS ALIVE!

The two people were deep in conversation. How could it have happened – an innocent man, God's Saviour, crucified? And yet some said that Jesus was alive. What was going on?

A stranger joined them, and asked, "What are you talking about?"

"Haven't you heard?" they replied, and they told him all about Jesus.

And then the stranger began to explain what the prophets had said about Jesus, how he would be killed, but would rise from death.

When they got to Emmaus, Cleopas and his wife asked the stranger to eat with them.

The stranger said a prayer of thanks, and gave them each a piece of bread. Then they saw it was Jesus!

The risen Jesus was seen by hundreds of people after his resurrection. "I won't believe it unless I see him," Thomas had said. When Jesus appeared to him, Thomas sank to his knees. "My Lord and my God," he said.

One evening Peter and his friends went fishing. By morning they had caught nothing.

Someone on the shore called out to them, "Throw your nets out on the other side." So they did, catching a huge number of fish. Then they recognised the stranger.

"It's Jesus!" shouted Peter, and leapt out of the boat.

In Jerusalem, the followers of Jesus were behind locked doors. They were scared – were the authorities coming for them next?

Suddenly Jesus appeared in the room.

"Peace be with you," he said. "Don't be frightened. Touch me."

When the disciples saw the scars, they knew it was Jesus.

"You are my witnesses," he told them. "I will send the Holy Spirit to help you."

Together they enjoyed bread and fish cooked over charcoal.

Jesus turned to Peter, who had denied he knew Jesus on the night of his arrest.

"Peter," said Jesus, "from now on, you must lead and teach my followers."

Peter knew he was forgiven.

The last time the disciples saw Jesus, he said, "Wait in Jerusalem, and I will send you the Holy Spirit. You will be given power to tell the world about me. And I will be with you always, I promise."

Then he left them, and went to be with his Father in heaven.

POWER AT PENTECOST

Jerusalem was packed with visitors – Jewish people from everywhere who had come to celebrate the Pentecost festival.

In an upper room the followers of Jesus were gathered. Suddenly the house was filled with the sound of a strong wind. Everyone seemed to be touched by flames of fire, as the Holy Spirit came.

When they heard the noise, a large crowd gathered outside.

The followers of Jesus came out, each talking in a different language about the wonderful things God had done.

Soon everyone in Jerusalem had heard the news.

"They must be mad!" said some.

"But they have found true happiness," said others. They saw how the believers shared their food and money. And every day, more people became followers of Jesus.

One day, as Peter and John went to pray, they saw a beggar who had never been able to walk.

"Give me some money," he begged.

"We haven't any money," said Peter. "But we will give you something else: in the name of Jesus, stand up and walk!"

Immediately, the man stood up, walked and praised God.

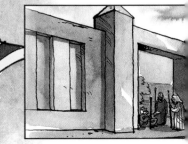

The people in the crowd were all able to understand what they said.

"What's going on?" they said.

And so Peter started to tell them about how Jesus had been put to death.

"And now he's alive!" said Peter.

The people were horrified when they heard how God's Saviour had been beaten and crucified.

"What shall we do?" they asked.

"Turn away from doing bad things, and follow Jesus," said Peter. "Receive God's forgiveness and the Holy Spirit."

That day, about 3,000 people were baptised as followers of Jesus.

Now the religious people were frightened when they heard of miracles and healings, and they arrested Peter and John.

"How did you make that beggar well?" they demanded.

"He was healed in the name of Jesus," Peter replied. "You crucified him, but he rose from the dead."

The religious authorities could not keep them in prison, so they were released. And the Holy Spirit gave them boldness to carry on telling people about Jesus.

115

A SHOCK FOR PAUL

"We warned you not to talk about Jesus!" shouted the high priest.

"We must obey God rather than men," answered Peter.

"Don't hurt them," said one wise man. "If this is really from God, nothing can stop it."

And nothing could stop the good news of Jesus spreading. The Holy Spirit gave Jesus' followers courage, even when they were in fear for their lives.

When Stephen was about to be stoned to death, he said, "Lord Jesus, forgive these people."

A young man called Paul watched Stephen die. Paul was very religious. He was sure God thought well of him. Now he was a man with a mission: to hunt down followers of Jesus.

But as Paul dragged Christians off to prison, hundreds more fled to other places, telling people about Jesus as they went. Paul then set off for Damascus to imprison any followers of Jesus he could find.

At about midday, a bright light flashed all around Paul. He heard a voice: "Paul, why are you persecuting me?"

"Who are you?" he asked.

"I am Jesus, and you are persecuting me," came the reply. "Go into the city. You will be told what to do next."

When Paul got up, he could not see. His companions had to lead him to Damascus.

In the city Jesus spoke to Ananias in a vision: "Go to Straight Street where you will find a man called Paul. He too has had a vision. You must go to him."

Ananias was shocked.

"Not Paul!" he said. "He's come to arrest us."

"Go," said Jesus. "I have chosen Paul to tell everyone in the world the good news."

So Ananias went.

"Paul," said Ananias, "Jesus has sent me to pray so that you can see, and receive the Holy Spirit."

Suddenly Paul could see again. He had some food and was baptised.

Now the news spread like wildfire. Paul's message was simple: "Jesus is the Son of God."

Soon the leaders in Damascus hatched a plot to kill Paul, and so his new friends helped him escape down the city walls in a basket.

"Please come and help us!" said the two men, arriving in Lydda.

So Peter and his companions set off for the busy port of Joppa, where he healed people who were sick and dying, and taught the new Christians how to live lives that pleased God. And more and more people believed, day by day.

While he was in Joppa, God spoke to Peter in a vision. Peter saw a sheet being let down from heaven, full of unclean animals, reptiles and birds.

When he heard God telling him to eat, Peter refused. He had always obeyed the Jewish food laws.

"Do not call unclean the things that God has made," said the voice.

While Peter was wondering what this meant, God said to him, "Three men are coming from Caesarea, looking for you. Go with them, because I have sent them."

118

Just then three men arrived.

"We are servants of Cornelius the Roman centurion," they said. "He is a God-fearing man, and he has had a vision."

The men told him that an angel had appeared to Cornelius, and told him to send for Peter.

The next day Peter set out for Caesarea.

Peter found a crowd waiting for him at the house of Cornelius. Suddenly Peter knew the meaning of his vision: God had made the world and everything in it; and the message of Jesus was for everyone, not just for Jews, but also for Gentiles.

As Peter told them about Jesus, the Holy Spirit came to all the people in the house, a sign of God's blessing. Peter was astonished. Now it was clear that the message of Jesus really was for everyone.

In Jerusalem, the believers were once more facing persecution. After James was executed, the Christians met in secret, gathering together in each other's houses to learn about Jesus and to pray.

The cruel King Herod Agrippa was in charge. He soon realised that he could get the religious authorities on his side if he got rid of the Christians.

So Herod had Peter arrested.

"Guard him carefully," he told his men, and planned a public trial.

Peter's chains fell off, and he followed the angel through the prison, until they got to the gate which led into the city. It swung open.

Suddenly Peter realised he was free, and standing in the middle of Jerusalem at night. Without hesitating, Peter set off for Mary's house.

Peter stood at the outer door, and knocked.

The servant-girl, Rhoda, recognised his voice straight away, and ran back inside to tell everyone, leaving him outside.

The night before the trial, Peter was fast asleep in his cell.

Suddenly, the cell was filled with light, and an angel appeared.

"Quick! Get up!" said the angel. "Put on your sandals and your cloak."

It was not the first time Peter had been flung into prison, and each night he slept on the cold floor, chained to two soldiers, with two more soldiers at the door.

Meanwhile, the Christians in Jerusalem were praying for Peter, their much-loved leader. "Please spare him, Lord," they prayed.

In the flickering lamplight, Jesus' followers were praying desperately for Peter's release. When Rhoda told them Peter was at the door, they couldn't believe it. So they went to look. It was Peter!

Quickly he told them what had happened. Then he left for a secret location.

The next morning, the guards at Herod's prison were in trouble, deep trouble.

And Peter was free.

Paul, once the greatest enemy of Jesus and his followers, was now one of the greatest leaders, ready to risk his life for Jesus. After a number of years with the Christians at Antioch, Paul set off on a journey, sent by God, to tell people about Jesus.

With Barnabas, Paul set sail for Cyprus, and then went on to present-day Turkey.

It wasn't easy. Everywhere they went there were arguments among the local people: some wanted to know more, and follow Jesus; others were angry, causing fights and riots.

Paul and Barnabas were now amongst Greek-speaking people with a different religion – the worship of many gods.

In Lystra, Paul saw a man who was disabled – he had never walked. When he saw the man had faith in Jesus, Paul said, "Stand up and walk!"

Immediately, people in the crowd started shouting, "The gods have come to visit us!" They thought Paul was Zeus, king of the gods, and Barnabas was Hermes, and so they brought garlands for them, and sacred bulls for sacrifices.

"No!" shouted Paul. "We're not gods – we're people, as you are. But we've come to tell you about the living God, who made the world and everything in it."

Then people who did not like the Christian message came and stoned Paul, leaving him for dead. The next day, he left that place.

On another journey, Paul took Silas, Timothy and Luke. They travelled by sea and by land, praying all the time that the Holy Spirit would guide them. Sometimes they visited places where there was a thriving church – a group of believers – to teach and encourage.

One night, Paul had a dream: a man from Macedonia in Greece was begging him, "Come here and help us." He knew this was a dream from God.

So they set sail for Greece, and went to the capital of the region, a Roman colony called Philippi.

Paul went down to the river, and began to speak of Jesus. A crowd of women gathered round, including Lydia, a rich woman who was a trader in expensive purple cloth.

Lydia was a Gentile who believed in God. When she heard about Jesus, she believed and was baptised, along with her family and servants. She invited Paul and his friends to stay at her house.

Philippi was a busy town, full of people who believed all sorts of things: Paul and Silas caused an uproar with their preaching, and were soon flung into prison.

Nothing could stop their joy in knowing Jesus, and so in the middle of the night they sang praises to God in their cell.

Suddenly, a massive earthquake shook the prison. All the doors flew open, and the prisoners' chains fell off.

The jailer was in such a panic, he was about to kill himself.

"Don't do it!" shouted Paul.

The jailer sank to his knees and said, "Tell me about Jesus and how I can be saved."

And so the jailer at Philippi and his family became followers of Jesus.

Next morning the town's authorities said Paul and Silas were free to leave. Paul travelled through Athens, Corinth and Ephesus, back home to Antioch.

Once more, Paul set out for Ephesus, with its marble pavements and many temples, including the famous temple of Diana.

He stayed there for two years, teaching and healing many people in the name of Jesus.

But not everybody was happy.

Paul had lost business for the silversmiths who made small statues of Diana for people to worship.

"These statues are not gods," said Paul, "they are made by man."

Demetrius, the chief silversmith, got the craftsmen together and soon a riot started, with people chanting, "Diana is great!"

When Paul returned to Jerusalem, there were more riots. Paul was again flung into prison, where God spoke to him, "Be brave! You will tell people in Rome about me."

Paul was imprisoned in Caesarea for two years before the order came to take him to Rome.

Guarded by a Roman centurion, and accompanied by Luke, Paul set sail.

The autumn winds were strongly against them and before long the crew could not control the ship. Paul tried to comfort the frightened passengers. God had sent an angel to tell him that the ship would be wrecked but no one would be lost.

Two of Paul's friends were grabbed and taken to the huge public theatre.

But the crowd would not stop chanting. Eventually an official managed to speak. "If Demetrius and his fellow-workers have a complaint, they must go to court," he announced. "Now go home!"

Paul returned by land and sea to Jerusalem. His friends in Ephesus and Caesarea somehow knew they would never see him again.

"I am ready to die for Jesus," Paul told them.

The next morning the ship ran aground near the island of Malta. The people there looked after the shipwrecked passengers until it was safe to set sail once more.

And so, at last, Paul came to Rome where he spent his days chained to a soldier.

But nothing would stop him passing on the good news of Jesus. From here he wrote many letters to teach and encourage Christians all over the Roman Empire; and many people came to him, eager to hear about Jesus.

125

Bible stories can be found as follows:

Published in the UK by Scripture Union
207-209 Queensway, Bletchley, Milton Keynes, Bucks MK2 2EB
ISBN 1 85999 497 0

First edition 2001

Based on an original text by Taffy Davies

Copyright © AD Publishing Services Ltd
1 Churchgates, The Wilderness, Berkhamsted, Herts HP4 2UB
Illustrations copyright © 2001 Chris Saunderson

Printed in Hong Kong